WICCA
QUICK GUIDE FOR PRACTITIONERS

A GUIDE WITH ESSENTIAL INFORMATION FOR ANY RITUALS AND SPELLS

JASMINE COOKE

Wicca - Quick Guide for Practitioners: A Guide with Essential Information for Any Rituals and Spells © 2020 by Jasmine Cooke. All rights reserved. No part of this book may be used or reproduced in any manner whatsoever, including internet usage, without written permission from Leirbag Press, except in the case of brief quotations embodied in critical articles and reviews.

ISBN: 978-1-7770364-1-6 (Paperback)
ISBN: 978-1-7770364-4-7 (E-book)

First Edition 2020

Published by Leirbag Press, an imprint of Virgo Publishers.
contact@virgopublishers.com

CONTENTS

INTRODUCTION 5

FRIENDSHIP 7

LOVE 11

MARRIAGE 15

SEXUAL ATTRACTION 19

PREGNANCY 23

MESSAGE / CONTACT 27

HEALTH / HEALING 31

PROTECTION 35

PURIFICATION 39

ENEMIES 43

LUCID DREAM	47
DIVINATION	51
MONEY	55
LUCK AND SUCCESS	59
BEAUTY	63
APPENDIX: MONEY AND LOVE SPELLS	67

INTRODUCTION

Whenever we need to create a new ritual or spell, we are faced with some doubts, such as which incense is right, the color of the candle, which herbs have the desired effects, etc. With that in mind, I have prepared this guide, which aims to eliminate all these doubts quickly and practically.

Wicca - Quick Guide for Practitioners is divided into areas, such as friendship, love, marriage, etc. Each of these areas presents the following relevant information: the spirits who can help us, astrology, items for rituals and spells, mantra, and Tarot cards. All this information can be used in magical works. I also provide a suggestion as to how you should proceed to achieve the desired result. Finally, in the

Appendix, you will find two exclusively money and love spells, prepared especially for you.

I hope that you, Wicca practitioner, find in this book the necessary answers to start or continue your magic in a practical but also effective way.

FRIENDSHIP

Spirits Who Can Help

Spirit	Title	Incense
Zeus	God	Frankincense, Oakmoss, Vervain, Sage
Raguel	Archangel	Ylang-Ylang, Magnolia
Mihr	Angel	Frankincense
Aamon	Demon (Marquis)	Jasmine

Astrology

Planet	Day of the Week	Color
Venus	Friday	Sky Blue

Items for Rituals and Spells

- Pink candle
- Incense: Frankincense, Cinnamon, Jasmine
- Honey
- Rosemary
- Sweet Pea Flower

Mantra

Om Hraum Mitraya Namaha
Om Eim Saraswatiyei Namaha
Om Eim Saraswatiyei Namaha

Translation

May the light of friendship shine through me, drawing noble companionship.

Tarot Cards

- ❖ Three of Cups
- ❖ Six of Cups

Suggestions

Reconciling a friendship takes time and patience. Don't try to rush things by casting multiple spells or working with various spirits at the same time. Have faith in your magical work, and wait for the results to appear. My suggestion is that you work with Aamon, as this demon has the ability to cause friendship between people. In addition, demons are known to be easier-to-work spirits.

LOVE

Spirits Who Can Help

Spirit	Title	Incense
Freya	Goddess	Nag Champa, Sandalwood, Mint
Aphrodite	Goddess	Rose, Frankincense, Myrrh, Vanilla, Cinnamon, Cypress
Eros	God	Rose, Myrtle

Hathor	Goddess	Myrrh, Cinnamon

Astrology

Planet	Day of the Week	Color
Venus	Friday	Sky Blue

Items for Rituals and Spells

- ❖ Candles: pink, red
- ❖ Rose petals and essence
- ❖ Incense: Rose, Lavender, Jasmine, Strawberry
- ❖ Apple, strawberry
- ❖ Cloves, cinnamon
- ❖ Sugar, honey
- ❖ Mead
- ❖ Rose wine

Mantra

May pure and true love appear in my life. May I love and be loved back.

Tarot Cards

- ❖ The Lovers
- ❖ Two of Cups

Suggestions

Love is a pure feeling that arises spontaneously between two people. It is not right to try to force someone to love you. Therefore, always try to attract true love, reciprocated love. One option is to work with Aphrodite on a Friday because she is also known as the goddess Venus, an expert on love issues.

MARRIAGE

Spirits Who Can Help

Spirit	Title	Incense
Hera	Goddess	Myrrh, Rose, Jasmine, Iris, Honeysuckle, Patchouli
Isis	Goddess	Myrrh, Sandalwood, Frankincense
Frigg	Goddess	Lily of the Valley
Jeliel	Angel	Benzoin

Astrology

Planet	Day of the Week	Color
Venus	Friday	Sky Blue

Items for Rituals and Spells

- Candles: white, pink
- Clove essential oil
- Incense: Sage, Lavender
- Holy water
- Objects that represent the union of the couple (marriage certificate, wedding rings, photos, etc.)
- Sparkling wine or Champagne

Mantra

Om Radha Krishnaya Namaha

Translation

Salutations to Radha and Krishna.

Tarot Cards

- ❖ The Lovers
- ❖ Ten of Pentacles
- ❖ Ten of Cups
- ❖ Four of Wands

Suggestions

If your marriage is experiencing difficulties, it is possible to solve them with the help of magic. But never try to force your husband or wife to do what they don't want to do. The goal of your magical work should always be to bring peace and discernment to the couple. Hera is an excellent choice of spirit to work with. She is the queen of the Greek gods and represents motherhood and family. Hera is always willing to help reconcile a troubled marriage.

SEXUAL ATTRACTION

Spirits Who Can Help

Spirit	Title	Incense
Aphrodite	Goddess	Rose, Frankincense, Myrrh, Vanilla, Cinnamon, Cypress
Eros	God	Rose, Myrtle, Frankincense, Myrrh, Apple
Lilith	Demon	Jasmine, Rose

Astrology

Planet	Day of the Week	Color
Venus	Friday	Sky Blue

Items for Rituals and Spells

- ❖ Red candle
- ❖ Red pepper
- ❖ Red wine
- ❖ Red rose
- ❖ Ginger
- ❖ Underwear
- ❖ Sex toys

Mantra

Om Kroom Lingaya Om

Tarot Cards

- ❖ The Lovers
- ❖ The Empress
- ❖ Ace of Wands
- ❖ The Devil

Suggestions

Sex magic is very powerful and can attract sexual partners into your life or improve your current relationship. One tip to enhance the effect of this type of magic is to masturbate during the ritual, but always keeping in mind that this is a sacred act. If you are a man, you can also use your semen as an offering to the spirit you are working with.

PREGNANCY

Spirits Who Can Help

Spirit	Title	Incense
Hera	Goddess	Myrrh, Rose, Jasmine, Iris, Honeysuckle, Patchouli
Isis	Goddess	Myrrh, Sandalwood, Frankincense
Taweret	Goddess	Frankincense, Myrrh
Freya	Goddess	Nag Champa, Sandalwood, Mint

Frigg	Goddess	Lily of the Valley

Astrology

Planet	Day of the Week	Color
Moon	Monday	Silver

Items for Rituals and Spells

- ❖ Green candle
- ❖ Incense: Apple, Floral, Jasmine, Marigold, Raspberry, Red Rose
- ❖ Crystals: Moonstone, Carnelian, Rose Quartz, Fluorite
- ❖ Essential oils: Geranium, Lavender, Rose

Mantra

Om Devki-sut Govind Vasudev Jagatpate
Dehi Me Tanyam Krishna Twamham Sharnam Gateh

Translation

O Son of Devaki and Vasudeva, the Lord of the Universe. O Krishna! Give me a son. I take refuge in you.

Tarot Cards

- ❖ The Empress
- ❖ The Sun
- ❖ Ace of Wands
- ❖ Ace of Cups
- ❖ Page of Cups

Suggestions

Prepare a ritual to be performed on a full moon night. If possible, do it outdoors on a day when the Moon is visible in the sky. If you have a partner, it may be a good option to include sex magic in the ritual.

MESSAGE / CONTACT

Spirits Who Can Help

Spirit	Title	Incense
Hermes	God	Camphor, Myrrh, Saffron, Dragon's Blood
Iris	Goddess	Iris, Violet, Lavender, Myrrh
Exú	Orixá (African deity)	Brazilian Cherry, Watermelon, Pepper

| Gabriel | Archangel | White Sandalwood, Ginseng, Camphor |

Astrology

Planet	Day of the Week	Color
Mercury	Wednesday	Purple

Items for Rituals and Spells

❖ Incense of any kind (incense smoke represents the air element that will carry your message to its target)

❖ Objects that represent communication

❖ Photo of the person

Mantra

[Person's name] will contact me as soon as possible. We will talk in peace and solve all the conflicts that exist between us.

Tarot Cards

- ❖ All Pages (cups, swords, pentacles, wands)
- ❖ Eight of Wands

Suggestions

Sometimes it is not possible to get in touch directly with someone we need to talk to. In this case, magic can help us convince someone to get in touch with us. Use the air element to carry your message to the person you want to communicate with. Be clear in your message and ask them to contact you as soon as possible.

HEALTH / HEALING

Spirits Who Can Help

Spirit	Title	Incense
Apollo	God	Cypress, Cloves, Cinnamon, Mugwort
Omolú	Orixá (African deity)	Camphor, Violet, Night-blooming Cereus, Coffee
Aladiah	Angel	Lavender
Mitzrael	Angel	Mint
Anauel	Angel	Eucalyptus

Astrology

Planet	Day of the Week	Color
Sun	Sunday	Yellow

Items for Rituals and Spells

- ❖ Candles: red, green, blue
- ❖ Crystals: Amethyst, Quartz
- ❖ Violet light
- ❖ Incense: Sage, Sandalwood, Frankincense

Mantra

Om Tryambakam Yajamahe
Sugandhim Pushti Vardhanam
Urva Rukamiva Bandhanan
Mrityor Mukshiya Mamritat

Translation

Let us worship Lord Shiva, who is holy and nourishes all beings. Just as a ripe cucumber comes loose from the branch that it is bound as soon as it ripens, let us be released from *death (from the mortal body), being granted the realization of the immortal nature.*

Tarot Cards

- ❖ The Sun
- ❖ Strength
- ❖ The Magician
- ❖ The Fool
- ❖ The Emperor
- ❖ The Empress

Suggestions

Always seek the help of a doctor for any health problem. Spiritual help should be used in conjunction with conventional medical treatments. That said, you can perform an energizing ritual with Amethyst, coupled with an environment lit with violet light, while you mentalize your body surrounded by flames of violet light. This combination is really powerful.

PROTECTION

Spirits Who Can Help

Spirit	Title	Incense
Zeus	God	Frankincense, Oakmoss, Vervain, Sage
Odin	God	Dragon's Blood, Pine, Sandalwood
Michael	Archangel	St. Michael the Archangel Incense
Lucifer	King, Emperor, Prince	Sandalwood, Lavender, Cedarwood

Astrology

Planet	Day of the Week	Color
Saturn	Saturday	Black

Items for Rituals and Spells

- ❖ Black candle
- ❖ Incense: Myrrh, Seven Herbs, Citronella, Dragon's Blood
- ❖ Garlic, pepper
- ❖ Plants: Rosemary, Rue, Dumb Cane, Saint George's Sword

Mantra

Aad Guray Nameh
Jugaad Guray Nameh
Sat Guray Nameh
Siri Guroo Dayvay Nameh

Translation

I bow to the Primal Wisdom.

I bow to the Wisdom through the Ages.
I bow to the True Wisdom.
I bow to the great, unseen Wisdom.

Tarot Cards

- ❖ The Hierophant
- ❖ The Star
- ❖ The High Priestess

Suggestions

To bring protection to your life, you can count on the help of one of the powerful spirits listed at the beginning of this chapter, combined with a bath of protective herbs like St. George's Sword.

PURIFICATION

Spirits Who Can Help

Spirit	Title	Incense
Hephaestus	God	Frankincense, Dragon's Blood, Pine
Apollo	God	Cypress, Cloves, Cinnamon, Mugwort
Loki	God	Dragon's Blood, Pepper
Baldur	God	Cinnamon, Frankincense

| Michael | Archangel | St. Michael the Archangel Incense |

Astrology

Planet	Day of the Week	Color
Sun	Sunday	Yellow

Items for Rituals and Spells

- ❖ Candles: white, gray, black
- ❖ Incense: Myrrh, Sandalwood, Peppermint
- ❖ Herbs: Guinea Hen Weed, Basil, Pepper
- ❖ Coarse salt

Mantra

Om Gam Ganapataye Namaha

Translation

Salutations to the Obstacles Remover.

Tarot Cards

- ❖ Death
- ❖ The Tower

Suggestions

All spirits mentioned in this chapter are rulers of fire or have fire as their element. Therefore, it is a great idea to use fire to purify any environment or your life. But this purification happens mentally, visualizing the fire element expanding and purifying the whole space. NEVER set fire to any material or object.

ENEMIES

Spirits Who Can Help

Spirit	Title	Incense
Odin	God	Dragon's Blood, Pine, Sandalwood
Michael	Archangel	St. Michael the Archangel Incense
Nelchael	Angel	Lavender
Hahahel	Angel	Chamomile
Malphas	Demon (Prince)	Storax
Haures	Demon (Duke)	Sandalwood

Astrology

Planet	Day of the Week	Color
Saturn	Saturday	Black

Items for Rituals and Spells

- ❖ Black candle
- ❖ Incense: Frankincense, Saint Michael, Eucalyptus
- ❖ Holy water
- ❖ Coarse salt
- ❖ Enemy photo

Mantra

Om Hleem Baglamukhi Sarwdushtanam Wacham Mukham Padam Stambhay Jihwa Kilay Buddhi Vinashay Hleem Om Swaha

Translation

Goddess, stop the speech and feet of all my enemies. Destroy their intellect.

Tarot Cards

- ❖ The Chariot
- ❖ Five of Swords

Suggestions

Perform a banishing ritual with the photo of the enemy asking him to go away completely from your life. Finally, burn the photo using the flame of a black candle.

LUCID DREAM

Spirits Who Can Help

Spirit	Title	Incense
Hecate	Goddess	Myrrh, Pomegranate, Mugwort, Cinnamon, Poppy
Hahahiah	Angel	Rosemary, Lavender
Lauviah	Angel	Benzoin

Astrology

Planet	Day of the Week	Color
Neptune	None	Black

Note: Neptune is undoubtedly the planet responsible for dreams, intuition, and psychic sensitivity, but it is not one of the seven major planets that govern our lives because of its distance from Earth. Therefore, it does not have a day of the week on which it rules.

Items for Rituals and Spells

- ❖ Silver candle
- ❖ Incense: Jasmine, Opium, Mugwort, Rose
- ❖ Crystals
- ❖ Essential oils: Rose, Sandalwood, Patchouli, Cloves, Anise, Rosemary, Cedarwood, Mugwort

Mantra

The next time I dream, I will remember that I am dreaming.

Tarot Cards

- ❖ Ace of Swords
- ❖ King of Swords

Suggestions

Before bedtime, light one of the incenses listed in this chapter. Then lie in bed in a comfortable position and begin chanting the mantra until you fall asleep. IMPORTANT: Place the incense in an appropriate fireproof container. Keep the room ventilated with the window open.

DIVINATION

Spirits Who Can Help

Spirit	Title	Incense
Hecate	Goddess	Myrrh, Pomegranate, Mugwort, Cinnamon, Poppy
Apollo	God	Cypress, Cloves, Cinnamon, Mugwort

Hermes	God	Camphor, Myrrh, Saffron, Dragon's blood, Cloves
Isis	Goddess	Myrrh, Sandalwood, Frankincense

Astrology

Planet	Day of the Week	Color
Neptune	None	Black

Note: Neptune is undoubtedly the planet responsible for dreams, intuition, and psychic sensitivity, but it is not one of the seven major planets that govern our lives because of its distance from Earth. Therefore, it does not have a day of the week on which it rules.

Items for Rituals and Spells

❖ Incense: Camphor, Jasmine, Mugwort, Rose

- ❖ Reflective objects: black mirror, bowl with water, crystal ball
- ❖ Tarot, Lenormand, Gypsy Deck
- ❖ Runes, coins

Mantra

Ong Namo Guru Dev Namo

Translation

I bow to the Infinite Intelligence and Creative Wisdom. I bow to the Divine Teacher within.

Tarot Cards

- ❖ The High Priestess
- ❖ The Moon
- ❖ Ace of Cups
- ❖ Four of Cups
- ❖ Ace of Swords

Suggestions

Divination requires psychic skills or complete mastery of divination tools, such as Tarot, for example. Try Lenormand, which is a deck with a smaller learning curve than Tarot.

MONEY

Spirits Who Can Help

Spirit	Title	Incense
Hades	God	Frankincense, Cypress, Narcissus, Mint, Pomegranate, Patchouli, Myrrh
Njord	God	Cedarwood, Vervain
Bune	Demon (Duke)	Sandalwood
Seere	Demon (Prince)	Cedarwood

Astrology

Planet	Day of the Week	Color
Jupiter	Thursday	Blue

Items for Rituals and Spells

- ❖ Green candle
- ❖ Incense: Cinnamon, Cloves, Patchouli, Jasmine, Vetiver, Vanilla, Pine, Saffron, Cardamom
- ❖ Plants: Money plant, Clover

Mantra

Om Shreem Mahalakshmiyei Namaha

Translation

Salutations to the great Lakshmi. May you pour forth your blessings upon me.

Tarot Cards

- Ten of Pentacles
- Six of Wands
- Nine of Pentacles
- Ace of Pentacles
- Wheel of Fortune

Suggestions

When we want to attract more money into our lives, there needs to be a source where the money will come from. So, always focus on concrete things, such as pay raise, a better job, an increase in sales of your company, etc. Asking for more money without specifying how this should occur can result in undesirable consequences.

LUCK AND SUCCESS

Spirits Who Can Help

Spirit	Title	Incense
Tyche	Goddess	Frankincense
Ganesh	God	Marigold, Jasmine, Lemon Balm
Lelahel	Angel	Roses
Lehahiah	Angel	Rosemary
Yelaiah	Angel	Fennel
Bune	Demon (Duke)	Sandalwood

Astrology

Planet	Day of the Week	Color
Jupiter	Thursday	Blue

Items for Rituals and Spells

- ❖ Green candle
- ❖ Incense: Lemon, Vanilla, Saint Expedite, Lavender
- ❖ Herbs: Oregano, Mint, Patchouli, Basil, Bay Leaf

Mantra

Chig Du Drol Chon Nu Nyid Chang Dam Pei Ne

Translation

Great Spirit of the Eight Destinies, give me the Quintessence of Infinite Luck.

Tarot Cards

- ❖ Ace of Pentacles
- ❖ Ace of Cups
- ❖ The Sun
- ❖ The World
- ❖ The Star

Suggestions

The first thing to do to attract luck and success is to remove the obstacles in your life. So, start by performing a cleansing ritual to get rid of all negative influences. On a Thursday — Jupiter's day — prepare a bath with the herbs listed in this chapter to attract luck and success in every area.

BEAUTY

Spirits Who Can Help

Spirit	Title	Incense
Freya	Goddess	Nag Champa, Sandalwood, Mint
Aphrodite	Goddess	Rose, Frankincense, Myrrh, Vanilla, Cinnamon, Cypress
Hathor	Goddess	Myrrh, Cinnamon
Jophiel	Archangel	Cloves

Astrology

Planet	Day of the Week	Color
Venus	Friday	Sky Blue

Items for Rituals and Spells

- ❖ Pink candle
- ❖ Lavender incense
- ❖ Pink Rose Petals
- ❖ Rose wine

Mantra

Om Padma Sundharyei Namaha

Translation

Om and salutations to She who personifies beauty.

Tarot Cards

- ❖ The Sun

- ❖ The Star
- ❖ The Empress

Suggestions

Prepare a bath with rose petals and light the space with pink candles. Write a conjuration calling for Aphrodite and recite it during the beauty bath. Perform this ritual on a Friday, the day of Venus.

APPENDIX: MONEY AND LOVE SPELLS

Money

In this spell, we will work with the god Hades, so all the items used are part of the nature of Hades. That's why we'll be using a black candle instead of a green one.

You will need:

- ❖ A black candle
- ❖ A bottle of wine
- ❖ Mint leaves
- ❖ Incense: Mint, Pomegranate, or Myrrh

❖ A plate or saucer

This spell must be cast on the ground. Do not ignore this detail.

1 - Place the candle in the middle of the plate, and the mint leaves around the candle.

2 - Light the incense and call the name of Hades for about three minutes.

3 - Light the black candle and then pour some of the wine on the ground.

4 - Make your requests to Hades in a clear and direct manner. Repeat it three times.

5 – Pour some more of the wine on the ground and thank Hades for having received your requests.

*Let the candle and incense burn until the end.

*There is no need to use all the wine in the bottle. The remaining wine, you can drink normally.

Love

It's not like me to teach spells to manipulate someone. But since I know that most people who look for "love" spells want to attract a specific person, I decided to include in this book a way to achieve this goal.

You will need:

- ❖ A red candle
- ❖ Jasmine incense
- ❖ An apple and some strawberries
- ❖ Red rose petals
- ❖ A bottle of red wine
- ❖ A glass cup
- ❖ Blank paper
- ❖ Red Pen

This spell must be cast between 3:00 and 4:00 in the morning.

1 - On a blank piece of paper, write down exactly what you want to happen between you and the loved one, including your name and his or her name.

2 - Place the candle in the center of the plate and decorate it with rose petals, strawberries, and apple.

3 - Place the glass and the bottle of wine in front of the plate. Leave the bottle open to easy the process.

4 - Light the incense and call the name of Lilith for about three minutes.

5 - Continue to call for Lilith while lighting the red candle.

6 - Pour some of the wine into the glass and offer it to Lilith.

7 - Ask Lilith for exactly what you wrote on the paper. Do it three times. Then burn the paper in the candle flame.

8 - Thank Lilith for her presence and remain silent for a few minutes contemplating your work.

*Let the candle and incense burn until the end.

*The remaining wine can be consumed normally.

www.ingramcontent.com/pod-product-compliance
Lightning Source LLC
Chambersburg PA
CBHW062155100526
44589CB00014B/1844